William Bolcom/Arnold Weinstein

CABARET SONGS

Volumes 1 and 2

for medium voice and piano

CONTENTS

Fifth Edition

Recorded on RCA-Red Seal record album LP HRCI-547 "Black Max"
The Cabaret Songs of Arnold Weinstein and William Bolcom.
Joan Morris, mezzo-soprano, and William Bolcom, piano.
Kerrytown Concert House, Ann Arbor, Michigan, February 14 and 15, 1985.
Producer for RCA: Sam Parkins.
Engineer: Don Puluse, with David Lau and Roger Arnett assisting.

Although **Cabaret Songs** were written for Joan Morris, technically a mezzo-soprano, these songs are intended to be sung in a "diseur or diseuse tessitura", that is, principally using the lower half of the approximately two-octave range of these songs.

 (the inner notes represent the principally-used range, the outer the rarely-used extremes)

This does not mean the singer should use chest tone exclusively! A more speaking tone is recommended in order to give the words equal value to the notes. (Bear the above in mind when deciding what transposition may be necessary.)

These songs are not written with operatic voice-classifications in mind, although they are performable by the trained voice and have often been so. Thus they can be fairly efficacious training in theater-style performance for voice students.

W.B.

N.B. — Accidentals apply only throughout a beamed group: but . In music with a key signature, traditional practice is observed.

What Is Cabaret Song

First, what it is not. It is not, like these notes, For Musicians Only. No piano tinkling unmerrily away out for an evening of no fun, especially for the words whose un-accented syllables are deftly fudged by accented accompaniment. As Lester Young said, "Play the words."

But what is cabaret song? Is it the long letter to the *Sad-Eyed Lady of the Lowlands* sung by sad Dylan or his commercial for psychedelics, *Tambourine Man,* or the John Wesley Harding dirge? Unh unh, them's western ballads sung in saloons of the Pecos, not in cabarets, though Jacques Levy's lyrics to Dylan's hymn *Durango* saunter easily into the cabaret spot.

Dylan's partners, the Beats, don't sit too well either in the cabaret's dopeless smoke. Ginsberg's blues remain cantorial, stoned. Maybe Kerouac's hip haiku joined Stan Getz in a successful debut of improvisational lieder that could be listened to in a kind of club. Jazz and poetry spent a lot of time hanging out in bars, but jazz and poems do not generally a cabaret song make. Fran Landesman is the huge exception, supernally talented writer of *Spring Can Really Hang You Up the Most,* to be hoarsely incanted in the dark to all the Sad Young Men at the bar.

Cabaret stuff cannot be electrified to an audience of teary old timers at the Palace or the kids at the Palladium nor yet to Felt Forum throngs. Maybe in a small concert hall but not really; that's more an experience brought about by the heartbreaking wear and tear of cabaret life on its ill-paid performers who need the occasional lucrative airing.

So what are we left with? Well, *aimez-vous* Poulenc setting Apollinaire's *Hôtel,* not wanting *travailler* but *fumer?* What about García Lorca's *Malagueña,* in which Death "enters and exits/in the tavern," like an O'Neill whore, sung in the long lines of flamenco? Or the Italian *Stornelli* sung table to table by wandering improvisors in Rome and Florence?

Despite Virgil Thomson's accusation that British ballads are ungainly, the snippy maestro and master critic might agree that certain poets certainly qualify as makers of the soft-sung poem that lends itself to cabaret rendering: Shakespeare, Jonson, Donne, Campion, Sydney, Blake. And Dryden gave Purcell plenty to sing about in the key of cabaret.

But it is in Germany that the rhinestone mantle of cabaret is worn most comfortably. Out of the Viennese café tradition that gave birth to Schubert's pop tunes, lieder in English, came the line from Oscar Straus to Brecht-Weill. Along the way, around the turn of our century, Schoenberg took time out from copying operetta scores to write a few dozen items called *Brettl-Lieder* — cabaret songs. (If you're lucky enough to find the record of Marni Nixon singing these you may be surprised.)

Brecht and Weill, vowing to "write for today, to hell with posterity," produced their immortal numbers under national conditions of stress, adumbrated in the stridency of their sound and image. The Brecht-Weill lyric rasping was played in all the Berlin clubs and has been played in all the theaters of the western world ever since; played and played since those fearful times because they wrote for that "today" that comes around again and again.

Cabaret likes such ideas. It was ears-on education for a Germany with an education limited to the few, and (even to those educated few) cabaret songs told much of what journalism left out. But the facts and notions taught in the sawdust classrooms of cabaret nite-life were collaged of poetry and flagrancy — not unlike the expressionist cinema of the day, nor the pre-postmodernism of Kurt Schwitters. And the lessons preached by Brecht of the preacher's family and the cantorial Weill were the doctrines of Einstein, Freud and Marx decked out in the lipstick and mascara of cabaret.

The idea of Ideas as kissing cousins of popular song might make some sense if you remember that Bacon, Harvey and Newton, Galileo and Copernicus were contemporaries of the same Elizabethan songmakers who gave us the innovations of sound and seriousness that characterize the lyric output of Dowland, Morley, Blow, Byrd. And though there were no cabarets at the time, there were taverns and street-corners and theaters where the small sound prevailed; folk and gentility met in the ballads that sang the news of the day.

The courtly and the popular were blended as early as the 15th century and wandered together with the *chansonniers* through the Renaissance. In *Marriage à la Mode* Dryden talks of notions "sung in cabarets," and Pepys in his diary (also of the 17th century) records walls that read *"Dieu te regarde"* in the French cabarets. So it seems that cabarets favored political salt and amatory sult back then too.

In our era Kaufman had a cabaret talent until it was gentrified by Moss Hart. Then the two emulated the courtly in their exclusion of the popular rawness and genius Kaufman had shown in his absurdist works 30 years before Absurdity. In our country Marc Blitzstein was solidly dedicated enough to have devoted serious musical energy to Saying Something. When asked why he tended to deploy his Schoenbergian background to sing of the unions, he answered, "Nothing is too good for the proletarian."

But the most daring moment in the history of cabaret occurred in Zurich in February 1916. On that day Dada was born; in the chintzy sleazy unartistic unintellectual atmosphere of the Cabaret Voltaire, the movement that was to transform modern art and lay the groundwork for post-modernism was announced by a reading by Tristan Tzara, followed by "performance art" by Arp and Kandinsky, lyrics by Wedekind, Morgenstern, Apollinaire, Marinetti, Cendrars. Designs by Modigliani, Picasso. Simultaneous reading of three poems "showing the struggle of the vox humana with . . . a universe of destruction whose noise is inescapable." (Hugo Ball's Diary).

An intellectually starved America, coming out of its long Puritanical fast, welcomed the new imports. Cabaret quality writing moved off the floor and onto the stage, where the '20s saw Rice's *Adding Machine* and Sophie Treadwell's *Machinal,* a kind of living newspaper that happened to star Clark Gable; in the '30s Rome's *Pins and Needles,* Blitzstein's *The Cradle Will Rock,* Weill's *Johnny Johnson* all had the episodic, collagistic approach characteristic of cabaret. Even *Our Town* has the spare, loose quality of revue, with the cohesiveness of real theme that makes it cabaretlike in form.

In England Auden had begun his campaign against the uncouth refinement of political rhetoric:

> *Stop all the clocks, cut off the telephone . . .*
> *Let airplanes circle mourning overhead*
> *Scribbling on the sky the message HE IS DEAD.*
> *Put crepe bows round the necks of the public doves.*
> *Let the traffic policemen wear black cotton gloves.*

Clear and simple, but demanding that imagistic attention characteristic of the cabaret experience. Auden also wrote such wry songs (to Britten's delicious music) as *Tell Me the Truth About Love:*

> *Is it prickly to touch as a hedge is*
> *Or soft as eiderdown fluff,*
> *Is it sharp or smooth at the edges.*
> *O tell me the truth about love.*

which, apart from the ironic (we hope) fluff/love rhyme, is like afterhours Cole Porter. But even the love songs of cabaret have a conspiratorial quality.

Thus, passing to the left, the Living Theater, the Open Theater, Caffé Cino; to the right, Bway and off-right, Off-Bway; in between was the Artist Theater (Koch, O'Hara, Ashbery accompanied by New York painters rather than musicians). And in some political bunker of their own architecting, a couple of writers met and wrote the songs on this album.

Norse-American William Bolcom the composer studied with Roethke the poet, and before that, his feet barely hitting the pedals, Bill had played for the vaudeville shows passing through Seattle with such songs in the repertory as *Best Damn Thing Am Lamb Lamb Lamb.* Milhaud found Bill and brought him back alive to highbrow music, though he never lost his lowbrow soul (neither did Milhaud). Operas later, we wrote these songs as a cabaret in themselves, no production "values" to worry about. The scene is the piano, the cast is the singer, in this case Joan Morris, who inspired us with her subtle intimations of Exactly What She Wanted. We hope she got it. Nobody defines better than she this elusive form of theater-poetry-lieder-pop-tavernacular prayer called cabaret song.

—ARNOLD WEINSTEIN

In addition to the *Cabaret Songs,* William Bolcom and Arnold Weinstein have collaborated on several projects, including the underground classic *Dynamite Tonite,* an opera for actors. Among Mr. Bolcom's recent compositions is a full-evening setting of William Blake's *Songs of Innocence and of Experience,* for soloists, choruses and expanded orchestra, which was premiered in January 1984 by Dennis Russell Davies conducting the Stuttgart Opera. Mr. Weinstein has written librettos for David Amram, Tony Greco, Oliver Lake, Laurence Rosenthal, William Russo and Henry Threadgill; his plays include *Red Eye of Love,* and *Metamorphoses* for Paul Sills' Story Theater. He is also a professor in the English department at Columbia University.

Over the Piano

Poem by **Arnold Weinstein**

Music by **William Bolcom**

Swoopy, with rubato: sentimental waltz-tempo

He sang songs to her _____ o-ver the pia - no.

Sang long songs to her _____ o- ver the

with a little more movement

pia - no._____ Low slow songs_____ lust-y songs of

hesitating

love._____ Lov-ing songs of long lost lust_____ just to

rit.

her just for her_____ o-ver the

a tempo

pia - no.

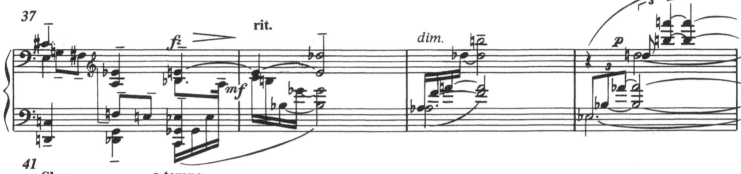

49

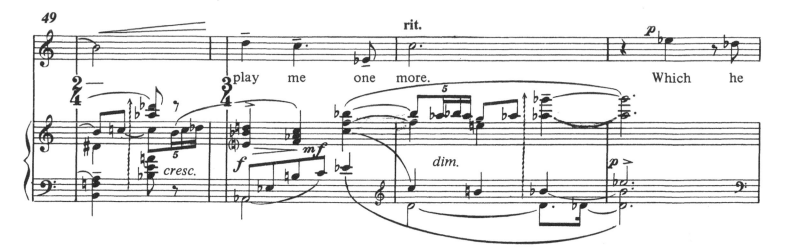

rit.

play me one more. Which he

53 a tempo

poco rit.

did and as he did Slid off the

57 a tempo

bench ___ and ___ said to her o - ver the pia - no ___ Good-

61 Slow; accel. Fast

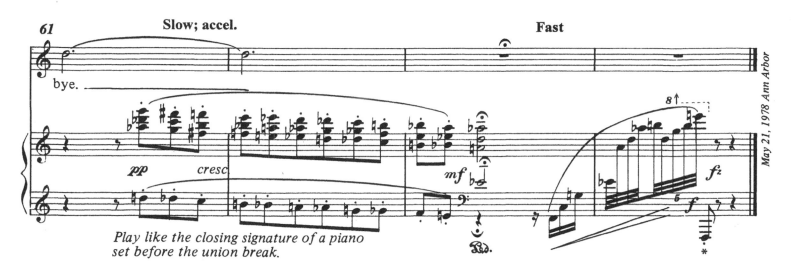

bye.

Play like the closing signature of a piano set before the union break.

May 21, 1978 Ann Arbor

Fur
(Murray the Furrier)

Poem by **Arnold Weinstein**

Music by **William Bolcom**

good and re-tired ___ now, ___ did-n't get fired, ___ now

ful - fils his de - si - res on half of his pay. ___

He eats in the best of dives ___ al -

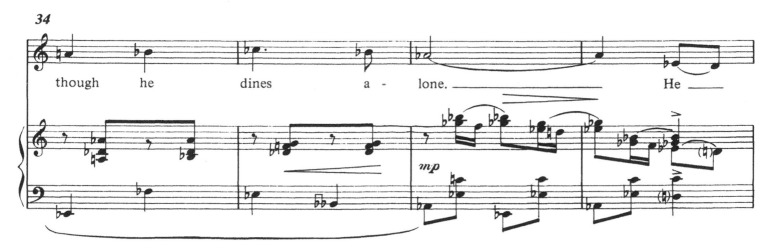

though he dines a - lone. ___ He ___

buried two won-der-ful wives _____ and he

still has the prin-cess phone. It's the

best of all pos-si-ble lives _____ own-ing all ____

that he owns ____ on his own. ____

56

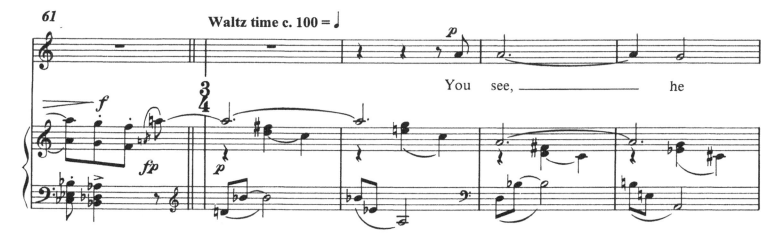

61   **Waltz time c. 100 =** ♩

You see, _____ he

66

ne - ver took off a lot,   and used to cough a lot,

71   **poch. rit.**

fur in his craw from hot days in the store.

Worked his way up to the top. Was the

stew-ard of the shop. Has a son who is a

cop and he is free! _____

My Un-cle Mur-ray the re - ti - ree _____ loves

this de - mo - cra - cy _____ and says it ve - ry em - phat -

ic' - ly. _____ He lives where he wish - es,

molto 2nd Avenue*

when he wants does the dish - es, _____ eats grea - sy k -

nish - es, _____ yes - sir - ree! _____

* i.e. with a slight growl.

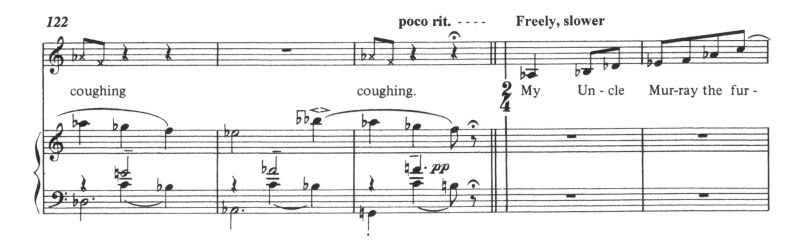

May 31, 1978 Ann Arbor

He Tipped the Waiter

Poem by **Arnold Weinstein**

Music by **William Bolcom**

pushed his but-ton so his gra - vy train

would glide a - cross the E -ly -sian plain

to Rome by night. I

Slow Polka ♩ = c. 72

met him on a Rom-an night and

then a-gain by Ven-ice light a - mong a flock of lat -est loves

Fast Polka

count - ing up his con-quests on grey suede ___ gloves ___ then shooed us

all a - way like tur - tle doves. And then he

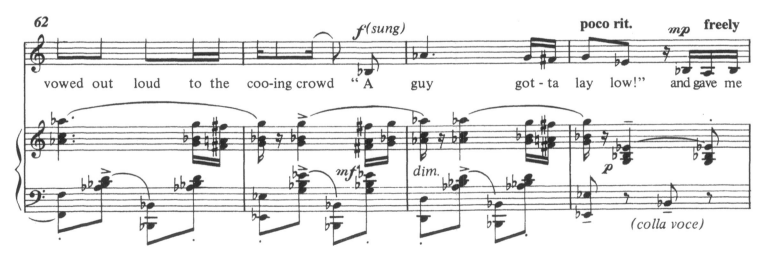

vowed out loud to the coo-ing crowd "A guy got-ta lay low!" and gave me

pause to re-a-lize _____ he would if he could _____ se-duce a ha-lo _____ the

great hole in the skies! His were not lies,

not mere-ly lies. Lies were his form of

mer - chan - dise.

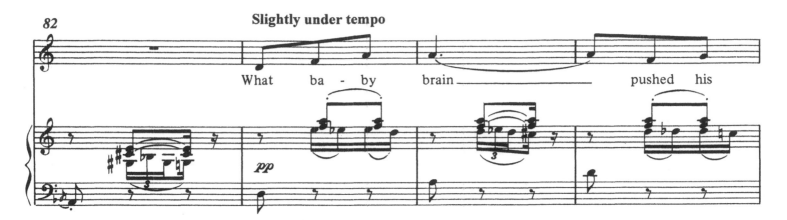

Slightly under tempo

82

What ba - by brain _____ pushed his

pp

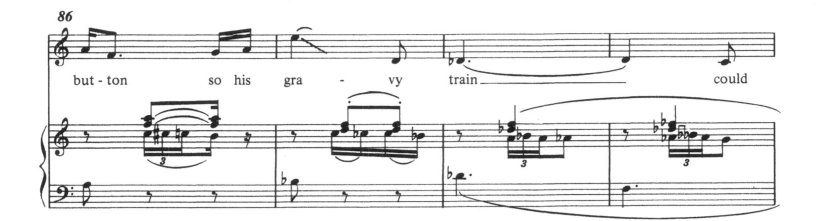

86

but - ton so his gra - vy train _____ could

90

keep on puf - fing a - cross the plain _____ to

legg.

ppp

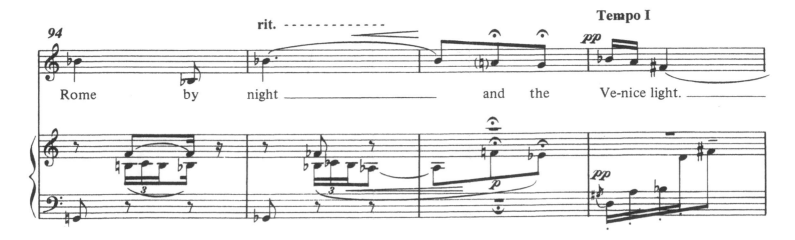

94

rit. - - - - - - - - - - - - - - **Tempo I**

pp

Rome by night _____ and the Ve-nice light. _____

p

pp

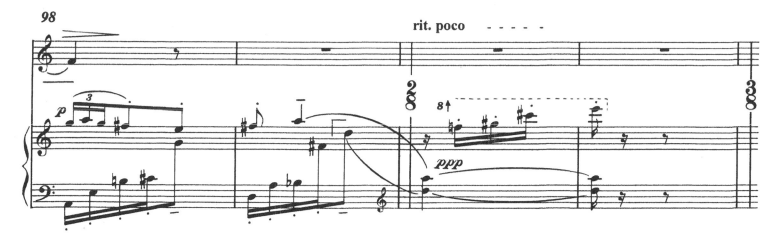

98   rit. poco - - - - - -

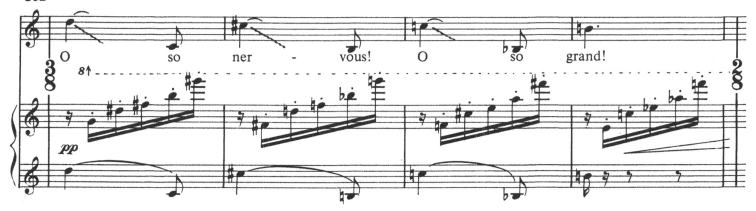

102   **Just under tempo**

O so ner - vous! O so grand!

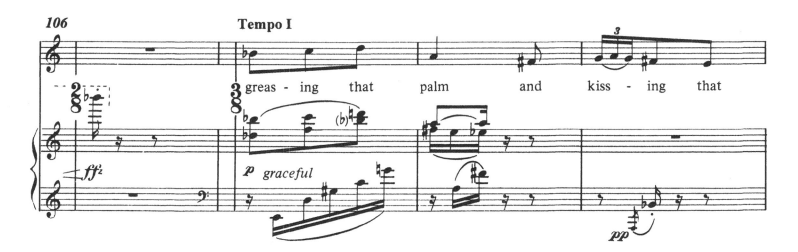

106   **Tempo I**

greas - ing that palm and kiss - ing that

110

hand.

October 1977 Ann Arbor

Waitin

Poem by **Arnold Weinstein**

Music by **William Bolcom**

January 4, 1978 Ann Arbor

Song of Black Max
(As Told by the de Kooning Boys)

Poem by **Arnold Weinstein**

Music by **William Bolcom**

17

of the town who raised their hats right back, nev-er knew they were

20

bow -ing to Black Max. I'm talk-ing a-bout night in ___

24

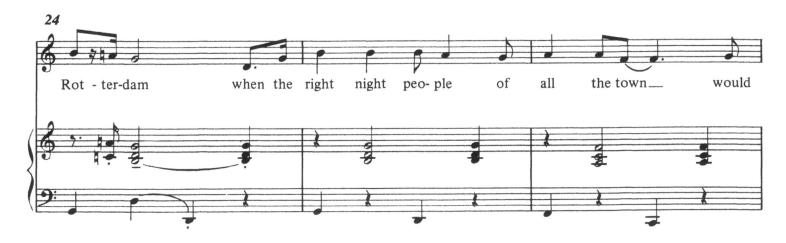

Rot - ter-dam when the right night peo- ple of all the town___ would

27

find what they could in the night neigh-bor-hood of Black Max.

There were wo-men in the win-dows with bod-ies for sale

dressed in curls — like lit-tle girls — in lit-tle doll-house

jails. When the wo-men walked the street with the beds up-on their

backs, who was lift-ing up his brim — to them? Black Max!

And there were looks for sale,___ the art of the smile,___

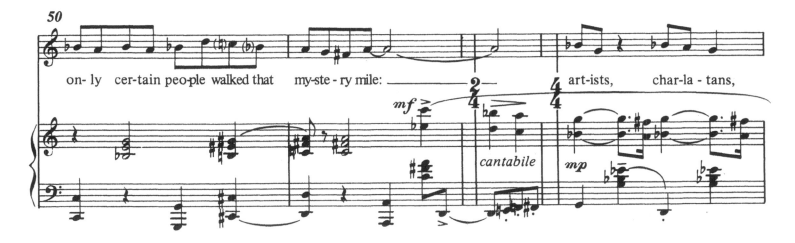

on-ly cer-tain peo-ple walked that my-ste-ry mile:___ art-ists, char-la-tans,

cantabile

vau - de - vil - lians, men of ma - the - ma - tics, ac - ro - ba - tics and ci - vi - lians. There was

57 *more and more spoken*

knit-ting-nee-dle mu-sic from a   la-dy or-gan-grind-er   with   all her sons be-hind her,

(mechanical)

simile

60 *spoken*   *(freely)*

Mar-co,   Vi - to,   Ben - no (Was he strong!   though he walked like a woman)

dim.

loud whisper

63

and Car - lo,   who was five.   He must be   still a-live!

(in time)

67 *spoken, in free time*

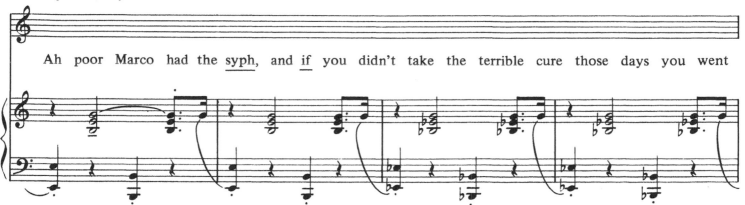

Ah poor Marco had the <u>syph</u>, and <u>if</u> you didn't take the terrible cure those days you went

un - der-neath the tracks. Stand- ing there be -

neath the bridge, long black jack-et, broad black hat,

play-ing the har - mon - i - ca, one hand free to lift that hat to me: ____

Black Max, Black Max, Black Max.

June 1, 1978

Amor

Poem by **Arnold Weinstein**

Music by **William Bolcom**

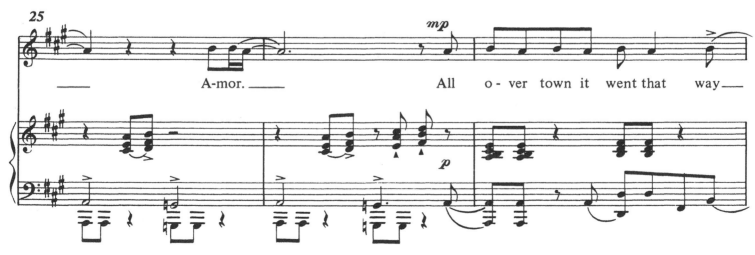

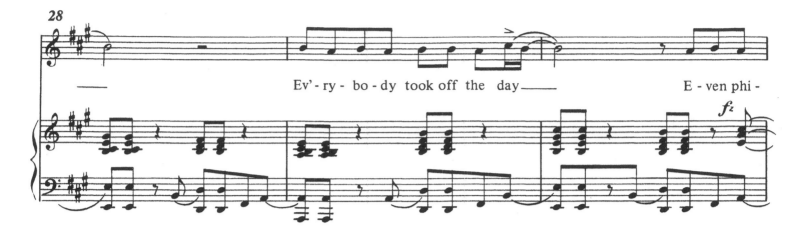

Ev'-ry - bo - dy took off the day___ E - ven phi -

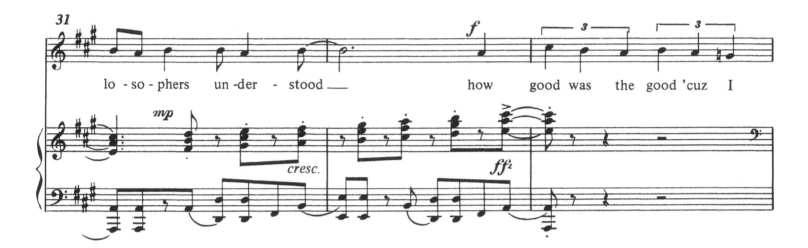

lo - so - phers un - der - stood ___ how good was the good 'cuz I

looked so good! ___ The poor stopped tak - ing less ___

the rich stopped need - ing ___ more. ___ In -

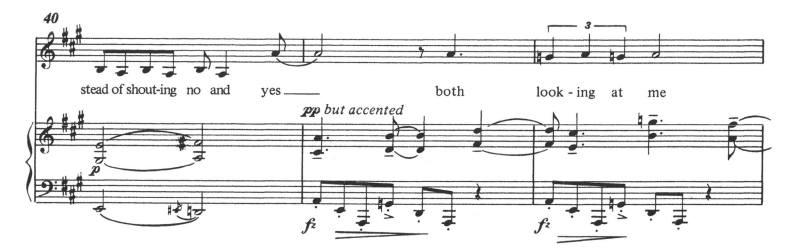

stead of shout-ing no and yes _____ both look - ing at me

shout -ed A- mor _____ Da de da (scat) _____

(Da) _____ (Da) _____

(Da) _____ My stay in town _____ was cut

short   I was dragged to court.   The

judge said I dis - turbed the peace and the ju - ry gave ___ him what

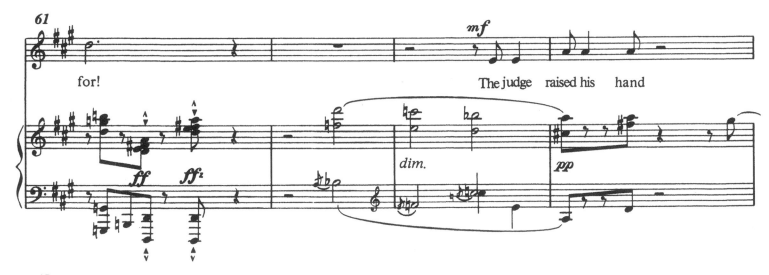

for!   The judge raised his hand

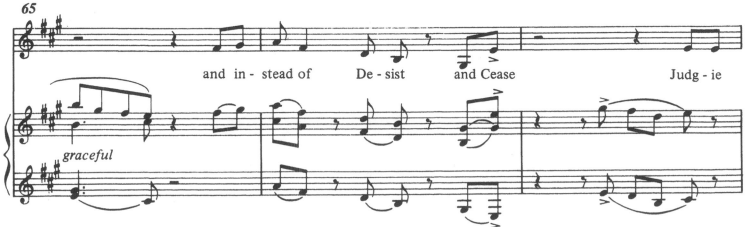

and in - stead of   De - sist   and Cease   Judg - ie

came to the stand___ took my hand___ and whis-pered A-mor

A-mor A-mor A-mor___

Night was turn-ing in - to day___ I walked a - lone___ a - way.

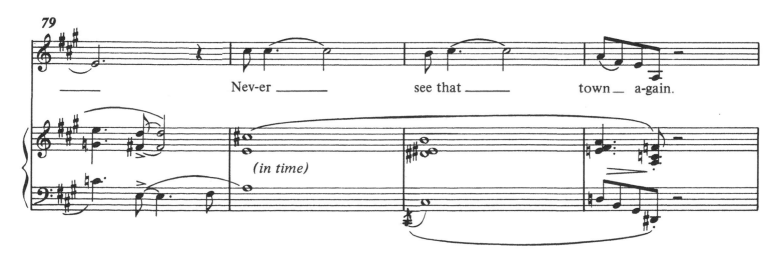

___ Nev-er ___ see that ___ town___ a-gain.

(in time)

January 11, 1978 Ann Arbor

Places to Live

Poem by **Arnold Weinstein**

Music by **William Bolcom**

Light, serene ♩ = 84

pp

una corda

(light touches)

simile

5 *p*

Pla - ces— to live! Give— me pla - ces— to live! Won - ders— to

10 *simile*

wan - der— to, pla - ces— to live! My feet are dream - ing— of

15

new dust,— new dirt;— my hips want— to swing in— a cel - lo - phane

skirt.   Give me my change in — a cel - lu - loid note while — I

buy wood - en hats from — the fac - to - ry boat.

Pla - ces — to live! Give — me

pla - ces — to live!   Won - ders — to wan - der to —   pla - ces — to

live! My ton-sils are long-ing to hum a new tune; I'm

dy-ing to dance by the dark of the moon With mus-tach-i-oed

mount-ies in deep pur-ple kilts and me in blue vel-vet on

flam-ing red stilts.

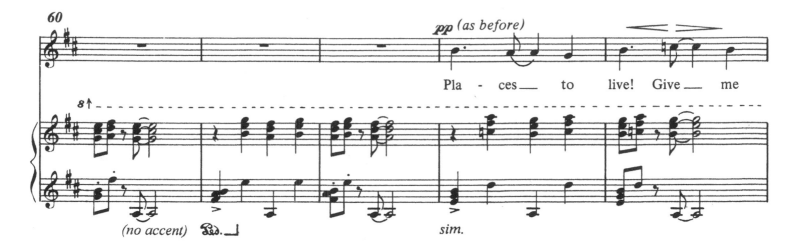

80

fea -thers— and give me re - lease, and— I'll kneel in— the sand and— I'll

85 *mf*

drown _____ my— va - lise. _____

molto leggero

90

Pla - ces— to live! Give— me

95 **poco rit.**

pla - ces— to live. _____

perdendosi

January 27, 1979 Minneapolis
Rev. February 11, 1985 Ann Arbor

Toothbrush Time

Poem by **Arnold Weinstein**

Music by **William Bolcom**

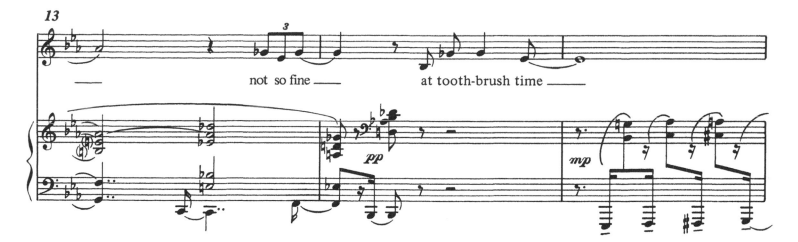

not so fine ___ at tooth-brush time ___

Now he's crash-ing round my bath - room ___ now he's read-ing my de-gree, ___

fast roll

sim.

pe - rus - ing all my pills ___ re - view-ing all my ills ___

___ and he comes out smell-ing like me. ___ Now ___ he ad-van - ces on my kit-

-chen, __ now he raids ev-'ry shelf

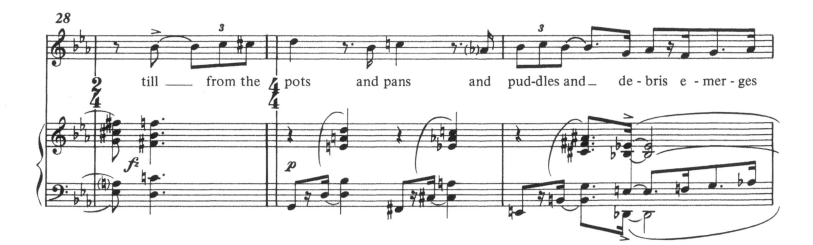

till __ from the pots and pans and pud-dles and __ de-bris e-mer-ges

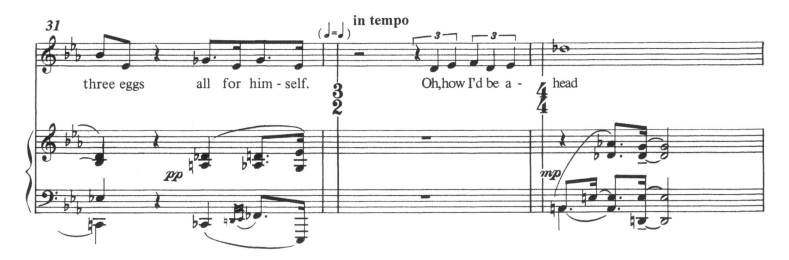

three eggs all for him-self. Oh, how I'd be a - head

if I'd stood out of bed; I would-n't sit __ here

grie- ving, ___ wait - ing for the won-der-ful mo - ment of his

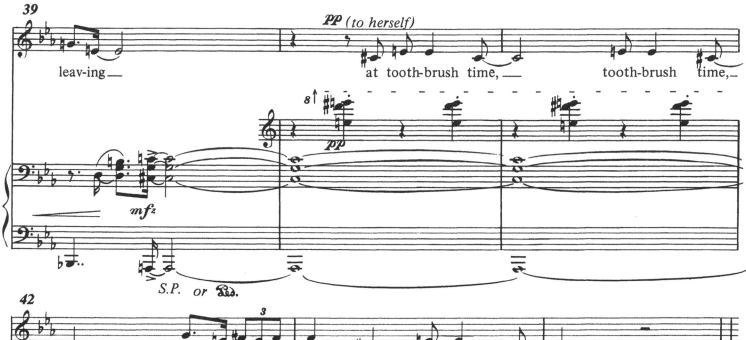

leav-ing ___ at tooth-brush time, ___ tooth-brush time, ___

PP (to herself)

ten a. m. a-gain ___ and tooth-brush time. ___

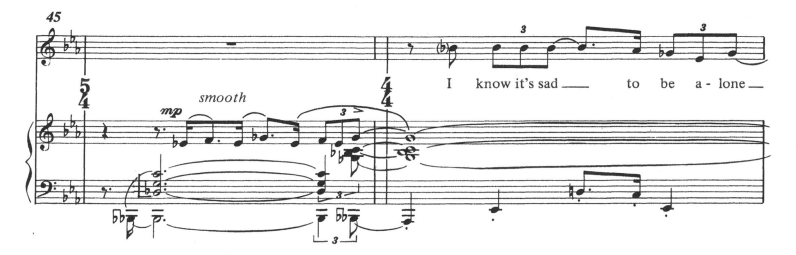

I know it's sad ___ to be a-lone ___

smooth

it's so bad to be a-lone,___ still I should-'ve known___

___ that I'd be glad___ to be a - lone.___ I should-'ve known,___ I should - 've known!___

Nev-er should-'ve picked up the phone

and called him.___

58 *spoken*

Hey - - uh, listen, uhm,   uh, I've got to, uh, - - - oh, you gotta go too? So glad you understand.
(trying to remember his name)

61

sung: freely (but enchained)

And - - - - - - - -   by the way,   did you

63   *rit.*

say   nine   to - night a - gain?   See you then.

Very slow

66 short *(disgusted)*

Tooth-brush time! ____

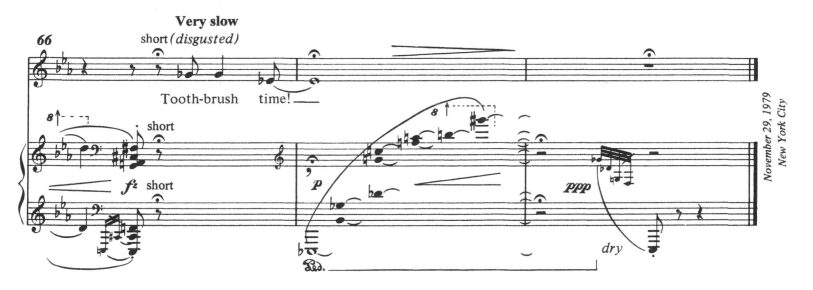

November 29, 1979
New York City

Surprise!

Poem by **Arnold Weinstein**

Music by **William Bolcom**

February 14, 1983 Ann Arbor

The Actor

Poem by **Arnold Weinstein**

Music by **William Bolcom**

ma - ti - nées from two to five to keep the show _____ a - live,

to keep the show a - live, dies for a liv-ing.

Seriously

I've tak - en the po - si - tion do or die! _____ not to sur-vive for

nor keep a- live for not to die for _____ a liv-ing.

February 2, 1983 Ann Arbor

Oh Close the Curtain

Poem by **Arnold Weinstein**

Music by **William Bolcom**

Slow Jazz Waltz Tempo

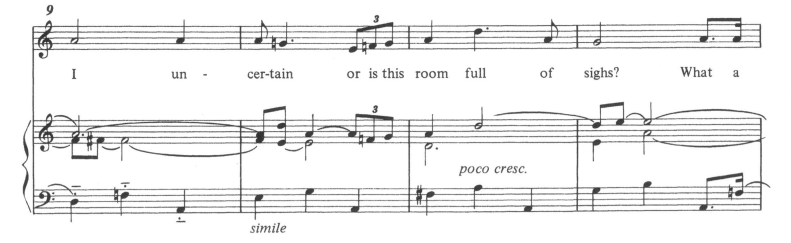

won - der-ful par-ty, ___ ne-ver heard ___ such lies! And

work toward tempo

More swung, in tempo
♩ = c. 96

oh I want so to be in with ___ these guys. _____

more 𝄢.

And there is more

drier

booze ___ than you could re - fuse, More do-mes - tics

no 𝄢.

pad-ding a-round _____ than you could e - ver lose, _____ But no one could find _____ my

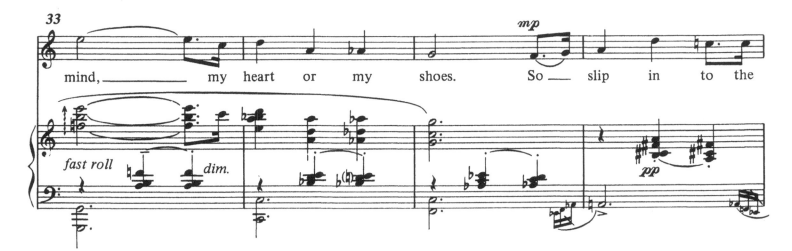

mind, _____ my heart or my shoes. So _ slip in to the

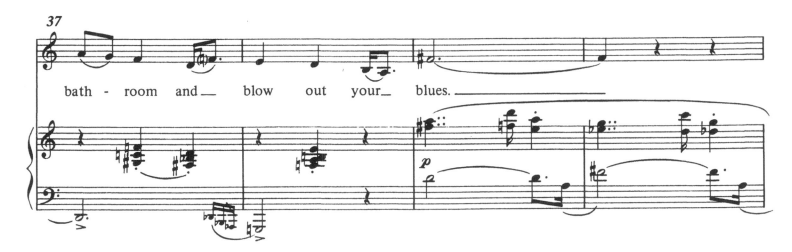

bath - room and _ blow out your _ blues. _____

Two

pa - ci - fist bro-thers are hav - ing a fight. A

wife's get - ting loose 'cause__ her hus-band is tight. Hear

mar - ria - ges break-ing all o - ver __ the night. And the

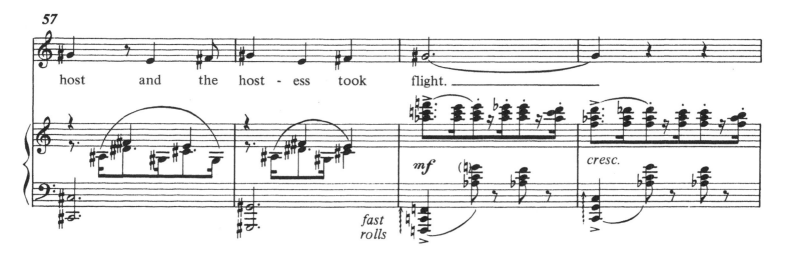

host and the host - ess took flight. _____

Oh don't close the cur - tain __ I

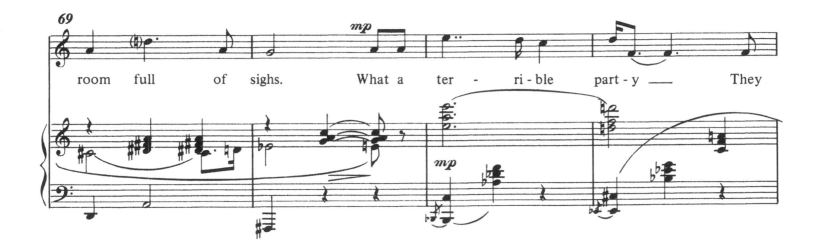

must see the skies. My heart is hurt in this __

room full of sighs. What a ter - ri - ble part-y __ They

ran out of lies. And oh I want so to be

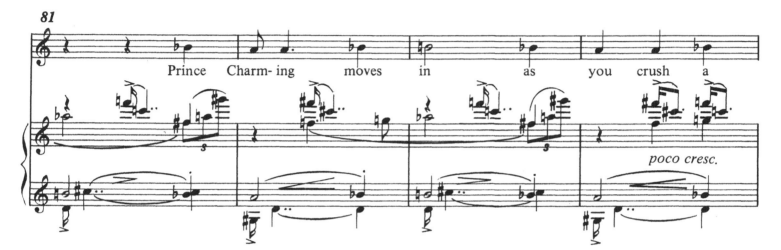

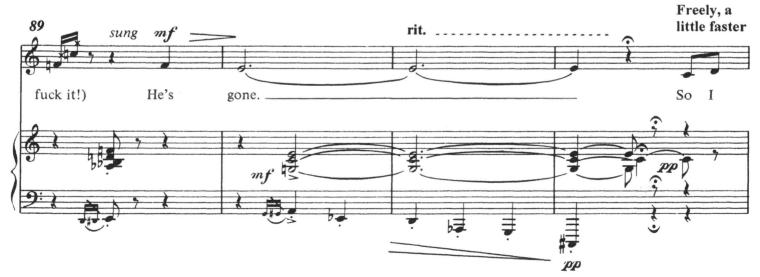

93

rit. - - - - - - - - - - - - - - -

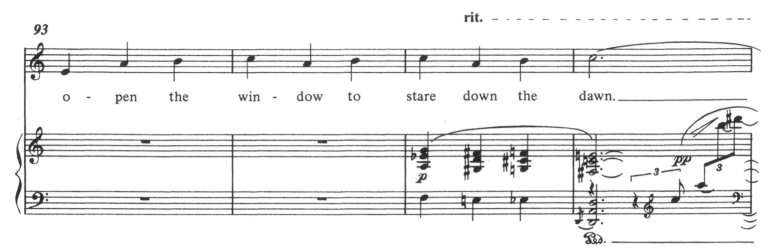

o - pen the win - dow to stare down the dawn.___

97

Very slow

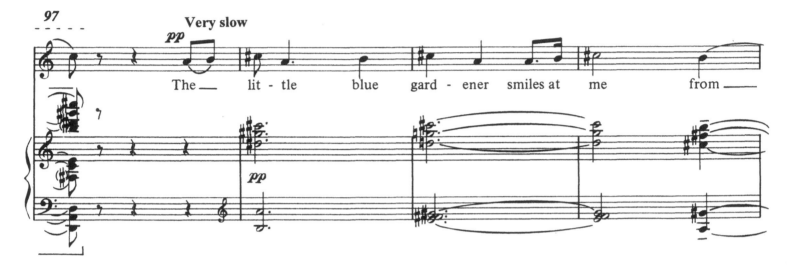

The ___ lit - tle blue gard - ener smiles at me from ___

101

Slow Jazz Waltz ♩ = c. 96

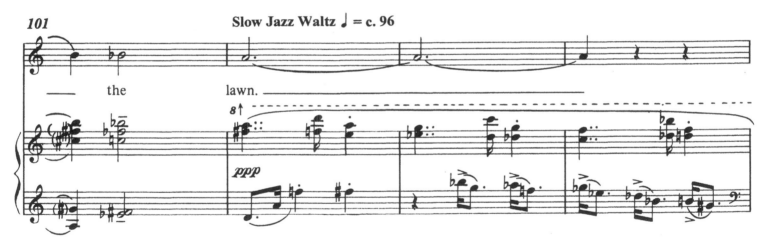

___ the lawn.___

105

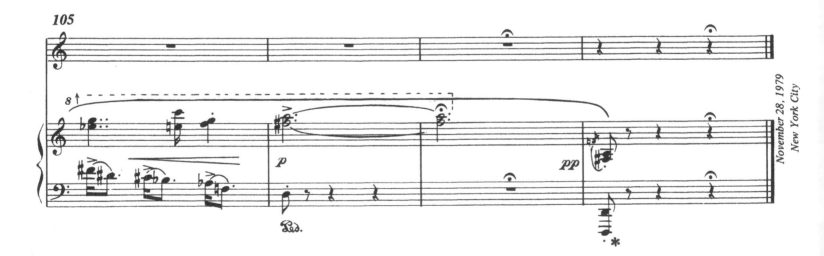

November 28, 1979
New York City

George

Poem by **Arnold Weinstein**

Music by **William Bolcom**

through__ the door he ne-ver locked__ and said, "Get your-self a

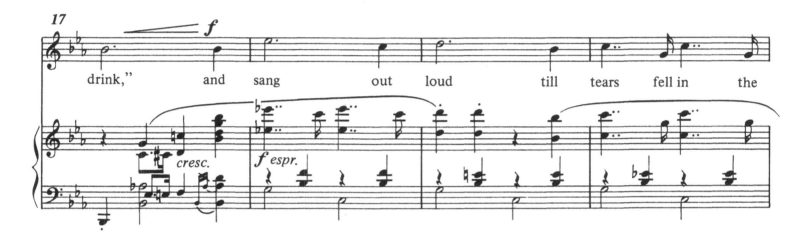

drink," and sang out loud till tears fell in the

cogn - ac and the choc' - late milk and gin and on the

beads, bro -cade and pins. When stran-gers hap-pened

through his o - pen door, George said, "Stay, but you got-ta keep

qui - et while I sing and then a mi-nute af - ter. And call me

espr., cantando   rit. - - - - - -   **a tempo**

Geor - gia."

One fine day a stran - ger in a suit of na - vy

41 blue took Geor-ge's life with a knife George had placed be-

44 *molto cantando* side an ap-ple pie he'd baked and stabbed him in the mid-dle of

48 *parlando* Un bel di ve-dre-mo as he sang for this par-ti-cu-lar

51 *poco rit. - - -* **A little slower** stran-ger who__ was in the U-ni-ted States Na-vy.

56 *freely*

The fu - ne - ral was at the cock - tail hour.___ We knew George would like it like that.

59 Slower and slower

Tears fell on the beads, bro - cade and pins_____ in the

62 *rit. -*

half-whispered

cof - fin which was white be-cause George was a vir - gin.

let off slowly   *

65 *(sung)*   **almost at tempo**   **poco accel. - - - - - - - - - - -**   **a tempo**

Oh call him Geor - gia, hon, get your-self a drink.

poco accel.

69
(singer portrays George silently)

73   **molto rit.**   **a tempo**

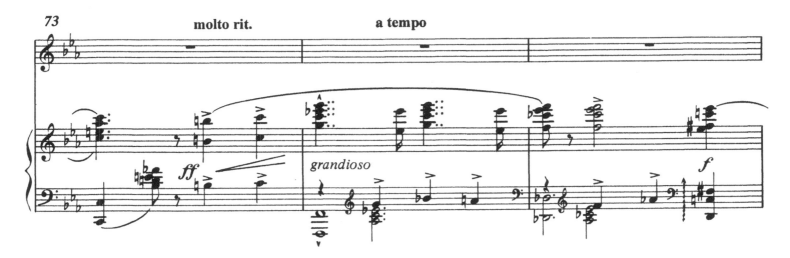

76

"You can call me Geor - gia, hon _____

79

get your-self a drink!" _____

August 13, 1981 Ann Arbor